THIS PLANNER
Belongs to:

_____

House Hunting List

ADDRESS	PRICE	NOTES

House Hunting List

ADDRESS	PRICE	NOTES

House Hunting List

ADDRESS	PRICE	NOTES

House Hunting List

ADDRESS	PRICE	NOTES

House Hunting List

ADDRESS	PRICE	NOTES

House Hunting List

ADDRESS	PRICE	NOTES

House Hunting Checklist

HOUSE SCORE:

PROPERTY ADDRESS

ASKING PRICE:

PROPERTY TAXES:

LOT SIZE:

PROPERTY SIZE:

FINISH:
- ☐ BRICK
- ☐ STUCCO
- ☐ WOOD
- ☐ SIDING

AGE OF PROPERTY:

NEIGHBORHOOD

DISTANCE TO SCHOOLS:

DISTANCE TO WORK:

PUBLIC TRANSPORTATION:

MEDICAL:

RECREATION:

SHOPPING:

ADDITIONAL INFO:

NOTES:

House Hunting CHECKLIST

DETAILED HOUSE FEATURES:

OF BEDROOMS: 　　　　　　　# OF BATHROOMS:

BASEMENT: 　　　　　　　　　HEATING TYPE:

PROPERTY CHECKLIST:

POOL ☐	BONUS ROOM ☐
GARAGE ☐	LAUNDRY CHUTE ☐
FIREPLACE ☐	FENCED YARD ☐
EN-SUITE ☐	APPLIANCES ☐
OFFICE ☐	A/C ☐
DECK ☐	HEAT PUMP ☐

NOTES

PARKING ☐
CLOSETS ☐
STORAGE ☐
☐
☐
☐
☐
☐
☐

NOTES

House Hunting Checklist

HOUSE SCORE:

PROPERTY ADDRESS

ASKING PRICE:

PROPERTY TAXES:

LOT SIZE:

PROPERTY SIZE:

FINISH:
- ☐ BRICK
- ☐ STUCCO
- ☐ WOOD
- ☐ SIDING

AGE OF PROPERTY:

NEIGHBORHOOD

DISTANCE TO SCHOOLS:

DISTANCE TO WORK:

PUBLIC TRANSPORTATION:

MEDICAL:

RECREATION:

SHOPPING:

ADDITIONAL INFO:

NOTES:

House Hunting Checklist

DETAILED HOUSE FEATURES:

OF BEDROOMS:

OF BATHROOMS:

BASEMENT:

HEATING TYPE:

PROPERTY CHECKLIST:

POOL ☐	BONUS ROOM ☐
GARAGE ☐	LAUNDRY CHUTE ☐
FIREPLACE ☐	FENCED YARD ☐
EN-SUITE ☐	APPLIANCES ☐
OFFICE ☐	A/C ☐
DECK ☐	HEAT PUMP ☐

NOTES

PARKING ☐
CLOSETS ☐
STORAGE ☐
☐
☐
☐
☐
☐
☐
☐

NOTES

House Hunting Checklist

HOUSE SCORE:

PROPERTY ADDRESS

ASKING PRICE:

PROPERTY TAXES:

LOT SIZE:

PROPERTY SIZE:

FINISH: ☐ BRICK ☐ STUCCO ☐ WOOD ☐ SIDING

AGE OF PROPERTY:

NEIGHBORHOOD

DISTANCE TO SCHOOLS:

DISTANCE TO WORK:

PUBLIC TRANSPORTATION:

MEDICAL:

RECREATION:

SHOPPING:

ADDITIONAL INFO:

NOTES:

House Hunting Checklist

DETAILED HOUSE FEATURES:

OF BEDROOMS: # OF BATHROOMS:

BASEMENT: HEATING TYPE:

PROPERTY CHECKLIST:

POOL ☐	BONUS ROOM ☐
GARAGE ☐	LAUNDRY CHUTE ☐
FIREPLACE ☐	FENCED YARD ☐
EN-SUITE ☐	APPLIANCES ☐
OFFICE ☐	A/C ☐
DECK ☐	HEAT PUMP ☐

NOTES

PARKING ☐
CLOSETS ☐
STORAGE ☐

NOTES

House Hunting Checklist

HOUSE SCORE:

PROPERTY ADDRESS

ASKING PRICE:

PROPERTY TAXES:

LOT SIZE:

PROPERTY SIZE:

FINISH: ☐ BRICK ☐ STUCCO ☐ WOOD ☐ SIDING

AGE OF PROPERTY:

NEIGHBORHOOD

DISTANCE TO SCHOOLS:

DISTANCE TO WORK:

PUBLIC TRANSPORTATION:

MEDICAL:

RECREATION:

SHOPPING:

ADDITIONAL INFO:

NOTES:

House Hunting Checklist

DETAILED HOUSE FEATURES:

OF BEDROOMS: # OF BATHROOMS:

BASEMENT: HEATING TYPE:

PROPERTY CHECKLIST:

POOL ☐	BONUS ROOM ☐	NOTES	
GARAGE ☐	LAUNDRY CHUTE ☐		
FIREPLACE ☐	FENCED YARD ☐		
EN-SUITE ☐	APPLIANCES ☐		
OFFICE ☐	A/C ☐		
DECK ☐	HEAT PUMP ☐		

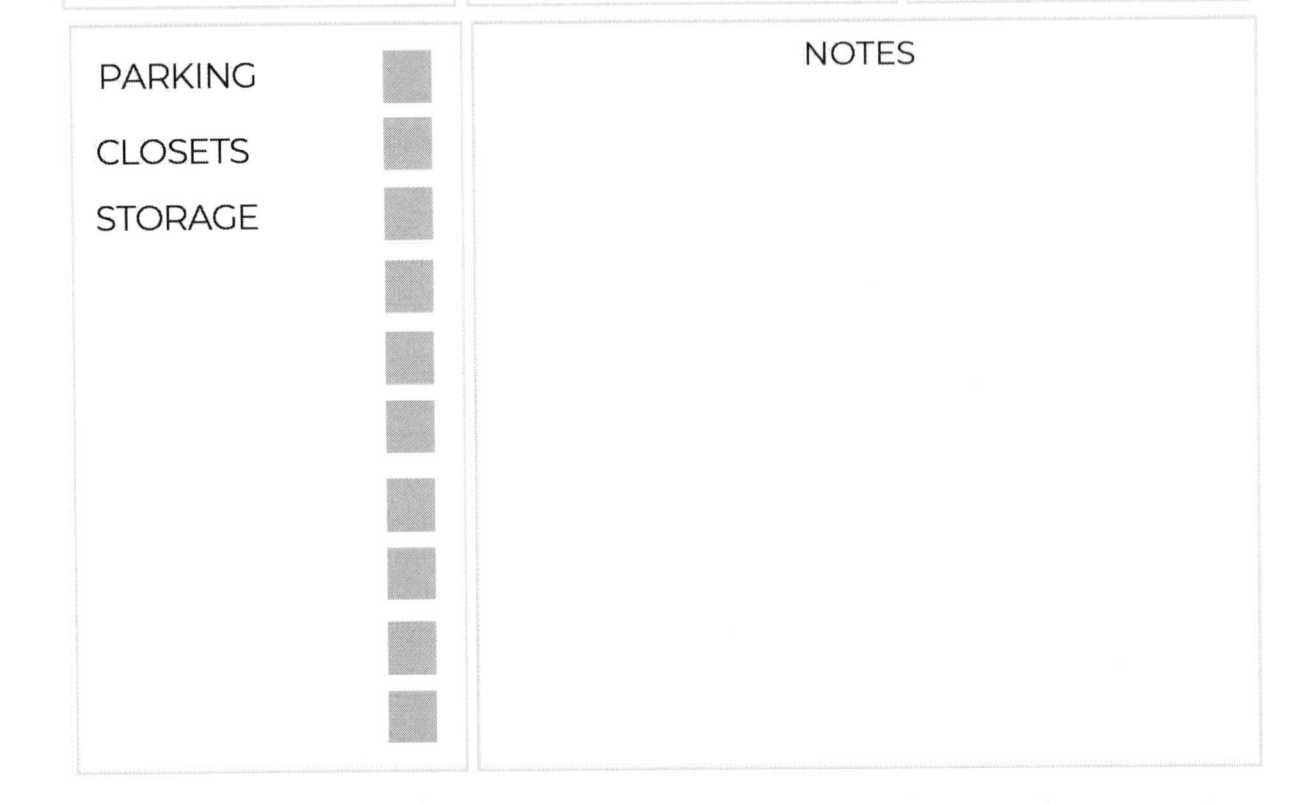

PARKING ☐
CLOSETS ☐
STORAGE ☐
☐
☐
☐
☐
☐
☐
☐

NOTES

House Hunting Checklist

HOUSE SCORE:

PROPERTY ADDRESS

ASKING PRICE:

PROPERTY TAXES:

LOT SIZE:

PROPERTY SIZE:

FINISH:
- ☐ BRICK
- ☐ STUCCO
- ☐ WOOD
- ☐ SIDING

AGE OF PROPERTY:

NEIGHBORHOOD

DISTANCE TO SCHOOLS:

DISTANCE TO WORK:

PUBLIC TRANSPORTATION:

MEDICAL:

RECREATION:

SHOPPING:

ADDITIONAL INFO:

NOTES:

House Hunting Checklist

DETAILED HOUSE FEATURES:

OF BEDROOMS: # OF BATHROOMS:

BASEMENT: HEATING TYPE:

PROPERTY CHECKLIST:

- [ ] POOL
- [ ] GARAGE
- [ ] FIREPLACE
- [ ] EN-SUITE
- [ ] OFFICE
- [ ] DECK

- [ ] BONUS ROOM
- [ ] LAUNDRY CHUTE
- [ ] FENCED YARD
- [ ] APPLIANCES
- [ ] A/C
- [ ] HEAT PUMP

NOTES

- [ ] PARKING
- [ ] CLOSETS
- [ ] STORAGE
- [ ]
- [ ]
- [ ]
- [ ]
- [ ]
- [ ]

NOTES

House Hunting Checklist

HOUSE SCORE:

PROPERTY ADDRESS

ASKING PRICE:

PROPERTY TAXES:

LOT SIZE:

PROPERTY SIZE:

FINISH: ☐ BRICK ☐ STUCCO ☐ WOOD ☐ SIDING

AGE OF PROPERTY:

NEIGHBORHOOD

DISTANCE TO SCHOOLS:

DISTANCE TO WORK:

PUBLIC TRANSPORTATION:

MEDICAL:

RECREATION:

SHOPPING:

ADDITIONAL INFO:

NOTES:

House Hunting Checklist

DETAILED HOUSE FEATURES:

OF BEDROOMS: # OF BATHROOMS:

....

BASEMENT: HEATING TYPE:

....

PROPERTY CHECKLIST:

- POOL ☐
- GARAGE ☐
- FIREPLACE ☐
- EN-SUITE ☐
- OFFICE ☐
- DECK ☐

- BONUS ROOM ☐
- LAUNDRY CHUTE ☐
- FENCED YARD ☐
- APPLIANCES ☐
- A/C ☐
- HEAT PUMP ☐

NOTES

- PARKING ☐
- CLOSETS ☐
- STORAGE ☐
- ☐
- ☐
- ☐
- ☐
- ☐
- ☐
- ☐

NOTES

House Hunting Checklist

HOUSE SCORE:

PROPERTY ADDRESS

ASKING PRICE:

PROPERTY TAXES:

LOT SIZE:

PROPERTY SIZE:

FINISH: ☐ BRICK ☐ STUCCO ☐ WOOD ☐ SIDING

AGE OF PROPERTY:

NEIGHBORHOOD

DISTANCE TO SCHOOLS:

DISTANCE TO WORK:

PUBLIC TRANSPORTATION:

MEDICAL:

RECREATION:

SHOPPING:

ADDITIONAL INFO:

NOTES:

House Hunting Checklist

DETAILED HOUSE FEATURES:

OF BEDROOMS:

OF BATHROOMS:

BASEMENT:

HEATING TYPE:

PROPERTY CHECKLIST:

				NOTES
POOL	☐	BONUS ROOM	☐	
GARAGE	☐	LAUNDRY CHUTE	☐	
FIREPLACE	☐	FENCED YARD	☐	
EN-SUITE	☐	APPLIANCES	☐	
OFFICE	☐	A/C	☐	
DECK	☐	HEAT PUMP	☐	

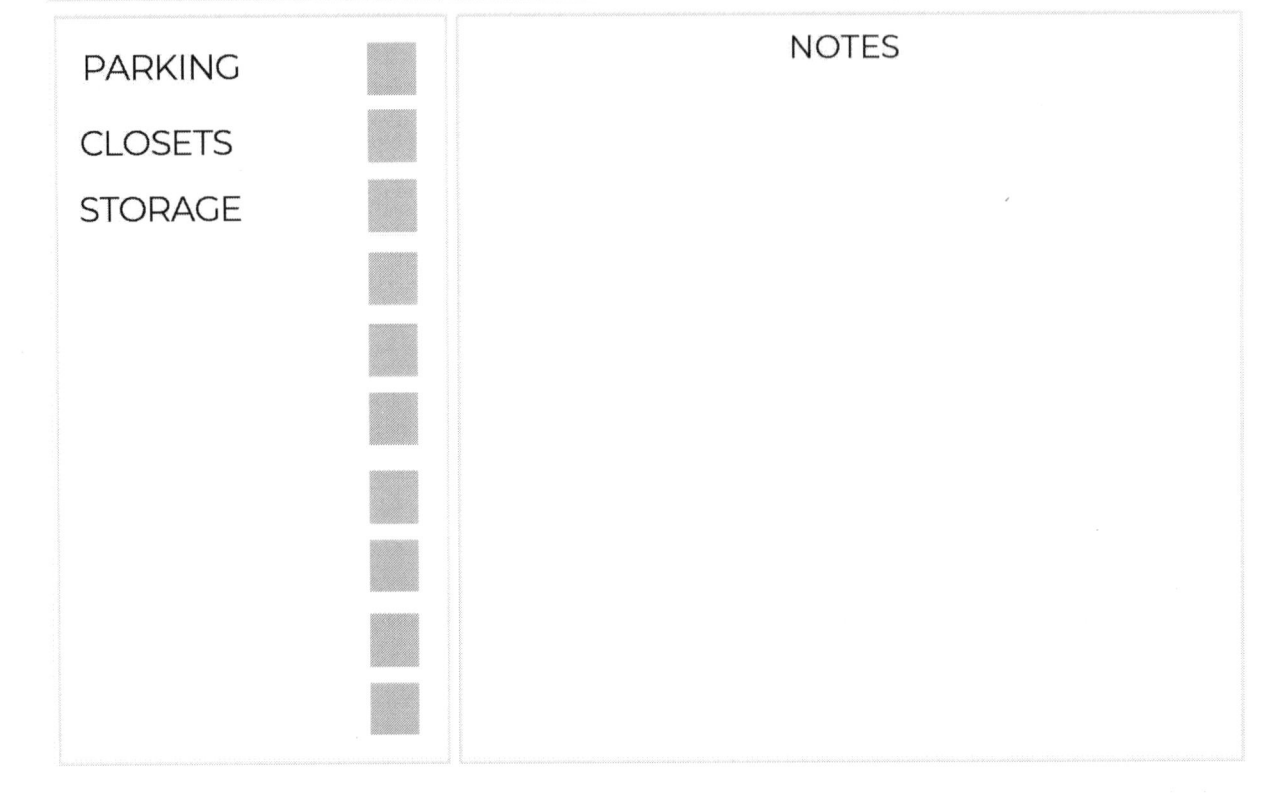

PARKING ☐
CLOSETS ☐
STORAGE ☐

☐
☐
☐
☐
☐
☐
☐
☐

NOTES

House Hunting Checklist

HOUSE SCORE:

PROPERTY ADDRESS

ASKING PRICE:

PROPERTY TAXES:

LOT SIZE:

PROPERTY SIZE:

FINISH: ☐ BRICK ☐ STUCCO ☐ WOOD ☐ SIDING

AGE OF PROPERTY:

NEIGHBORHOOD

DISTANCE TO SCHOOLS:

DISTANCE TO WORK:

PUBLIC TRANSPORTATION:

MEDICAL:

RECREATION:

SHOPPING:

ADDITIONAL INFO:

NOTES:

House Hunting Checklist

DETAILED HOUSE FEATURES:

OF BEDROOMS: .... # OF BATHROOMS: ....

BASEMENT: .... HEATING TYPE: ....

PROPERTY CHECKLIST:

- POOL ☐
- GARAGE ☐
- FIREPLACE ☐
- EN-SUITE ☐
- OFFICE ☐
- DECK ☐

- BONUS ROOM ☐
- LAUNDRY CHUTE ☐
- FENCED YARD ☐
- APPLIANCES ☐
- A/C ☐
- HEAT PUMP ☐

NOTES

- PARKING ☐
- CLOSETS ☐
- STORAGE ☐
- ☐
- ☐
- ☐
- ☐
- ☐
- ☐
- ☐

NOTES

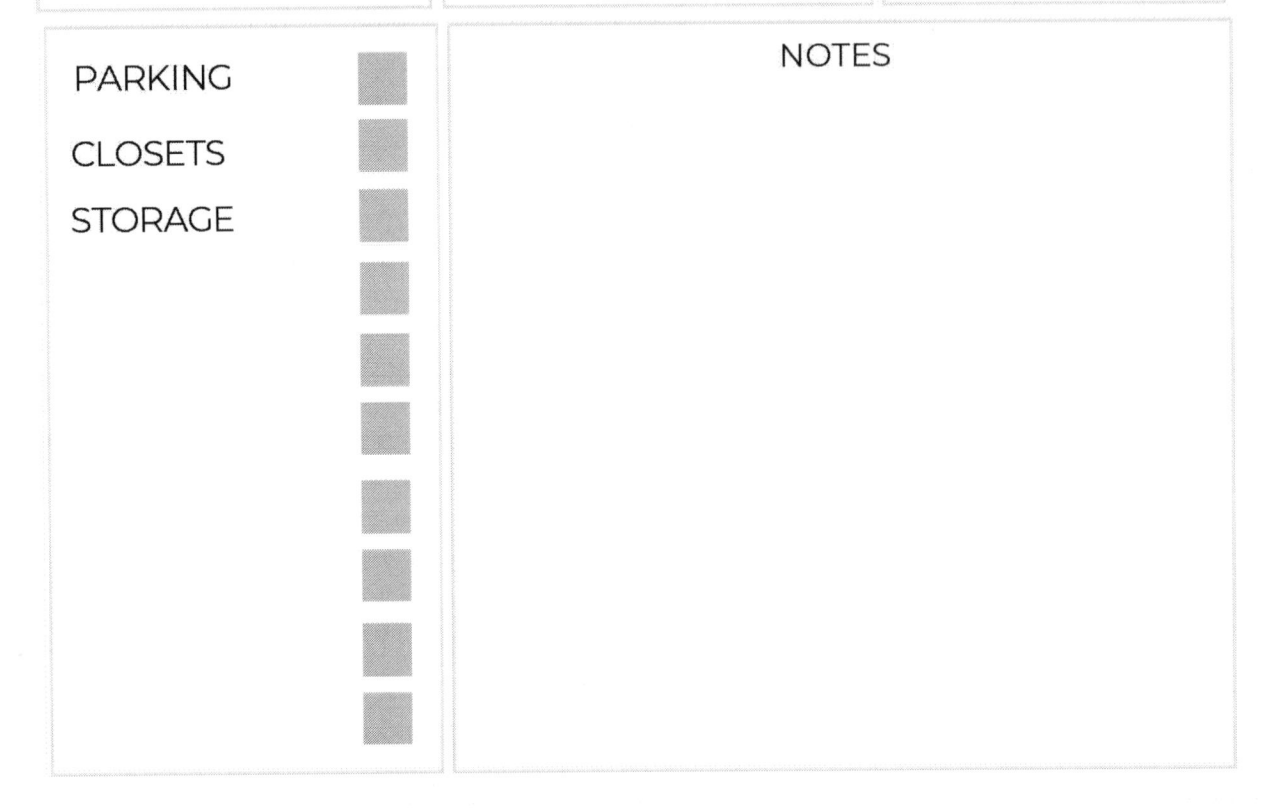

Budget & Expenses

PREVIOUS RESIDENCE

EXPENSES	BUDGET	ACTUAL	DIFFERENCE

NEW RESIDENCE

EXPENSES	BUDGET	ACTUAL	DIFFERENCE

OTHER

EXPENSES	BUDGET	ACTUAL	DIFFERENCE

House Hunting NOTES

House Hunting Notes

House Hunting NOTES

House Hunting NOTES

House Hunting NOTES

House Hunting NOTES

House Hunting NOTES

Address Information

PREVIOUS ADDRESS:

REALTOR:

- NAME:
- AGENCY:
- PHONE:
- EMAIL:

CLOSING DATE:

DATE:

PREVIOUS ADDRESS:

REALTOR:

- NAME:
- AGENCY:
- PHONE:
- EMAIL:

CLOSING DATE:

DATE:

NOTES & REMINDERS

Important Contacts

CLOSING ATTORNEY

NAME:
ADDRESS:
✉ **EMAIL:**
📞 **PHONE:**

MORTGAGE BROKER / COMPANY

NAME:
ADDRESS:
✉ **EMAIL:**
📞 **PHONE:**

MOVING COMPANY

NAME:
ADDRESS:
✉ **EMAIL:**
📞 **PHONE:**

HOME APPRAISER

NAME:
ADDRESS:
✉ **EMAIL:**
📞 **PHONE:**

NOTES & REMINDERS

Important Dates

MONTH:

NOTES & REMINDERS

Property Inspection Checklist

EXTERIOR CONDITION:	GOOD	OK	BAD
EXTERIOR OF PROPERTY			
FRONT DOOR			
PORCH/DECK/PATIO			
DRIVEWAY			
GARAGE DOORS			
OUTDOOR LIGHTING			
PAINT & TRIM			
WINDOWS			
WALKWAY			

NOTES:

ROOF CONDITION:	GOOD	OK	BAD
CHIMNEY			
GUTTERS & DOWNSPOUTS			
SOFITS & FASCIA			
YEAR ROOF WAS REPLACED:			

NOTES:

GARAGE CONDITION:	GOOD	OK	BAD
CEILING			
DOORS			
FLOORS & WALLS			
YEAR DOOR OPENERS WERE REPLACED:			

NOTES:

YARD CONDITION:	GOOD	OK	BAD
DRAINAGE			
FENCES & GATES			
RETAINING WALL			
SPRINKLER SYSTEM			

NOTES:

Property Inspection Checklist

OTHER IMPORTANT AREAS:	GOOD	OK	BAD
FOUNDATION			
MASONRY VENEERS			
EXTERIOR PAINT			
STORM WINDOWS			
PLUMBING			
ELECTRICAL OUTLETS			
FLOORING IN ROOMS			
WOOD TRIM			
FIREPLACE			

NOTES:

KITCHEN CONDITION:	GOOD	OK	BAD
WORKING EXHAUST FAN			
NO LEAKS IN PIPES			
APPLIANCES OPERATE			
OTHER:			

NOTES:

BATHROOM CONDITION:	GOOD	OK	BAD
PROPER DRAINAGE			
NO LEAKS IN PIPES			
CAULKING IN GOOD SHAPE			
TILES ARE SECURE			

NOTES:

MISC:	GOOD	OK	BAD
SMOKE & CARBON DETECTORS			
STAIRWAY TREADS SOLID			
STAIR HANDRAILS INSTALLED			
OTHER:			
OTHER:			
OTHER:			

NOTES:

To Do: Previous RESIDENCE

DATE:

MOST IMPORTANT

NOTES:

To Do: New Residence

DATE:

MOST IMPORTANT

NOTES:

Important Dates

Month

Notes

Moving Day List

OLD RESIDENCE	NEW RESIDENCE

Moving Day List

OLD RESIDENCE	NEW RESIDENCE

Moving Day LIST

OLD RESIDENCE

NEW RESIDENCE

Packing Notes

Packing Notes

Packing Notes

Packing Notes

Moving Day Planner

6-Weeks Prior

- [ ]
- [ ]
- [ ]
- [ ]
- [ ]
- [ ]
- [ ]
- [ ]
- [ ]
- [ ]
- [ ]

4-Weeks Prior

- [ ]
- [ ]
- [ ]
- [ ]
- [ ]
- [ ]
- [ ]
- [ ]

2-Weeks Prior

- [ ]
- [ ]
- [ ]
- [ ]
- [ ]

Moving Day PLANNER

WEEK OF MOVE

- [ ]
- [ ]
- [ ]
- [ ]
- [ ]
- [ ]
- [ ]
- [ ]
- [ ]

MOVING DAY

- [ ]
- [ ]
- [ ]
- [ ]
- [ ]
- [ ]

NOTES & REMINDERS

Moving Day Planner

PRIORITIES

MOVING DAY TO DO LIST

ORGANIZATION

MOVING DAY SCHEDULE

6 AM	
7 AM	
8 AM	
9 AM	
10 AM	
11 AM	
12 PM	
1 PM	
2 PM	
3 PM	
4 PM	
5 PM	
6 PM	
7 PM	
8 PM	
9 PM	
10 PM	
11 PM	
12 AM	

REMINDERS

Moving Day Planner

6-WEEKS PRIOR

- [ ] HIRE A MOVING COMPANY
- [ ] KEEP RECEIPTS FOR TAX PURPOSES
- [ ] DETERMINE A BUDGET FOR MOVING EXPENSES
- [ ] ORGANIZE INVENTORY
- [ ] GET PACKING BOXES & LABELS
- [ ] PURGE / GIVE AWAY / SELL UNWANTED ITEMS
- [ ] CREATE AN INVENTORY SHEET OF ITEMS & BOXES
- [ ] RESEARCH SCHOOLS FOR YOUR CHILDREN
- [ ] PLAN A GARAGE SALE TO UNLOAD UNWANTED ITEMS

4-WEEKS PRIOR

- [ ] CONFIRM DATES WITH MOVING COMPANY
- [ ] RESEARCH YOUR NEW COMMUNITY
- [ ] START PACKING BOXES
- [ ] PURCHASE MOVING INSURANCE
- [ ] ORGANIZE FINANCIAL & LEGAL DOCUMENTS IN ONE PLACE
- [ ] FIND SNOW REMOVAL OR LANDSCAPE SERVICE FOR NEW RESIDENCE
- [ ] RESEARCH NEW DOCTOR, DENTIST, VETERNARIAN, ETC

2-WEEKS PRIOR

- [ ] PLAN FOR PET TRANSPORT DURING MOVE
- [ ] SET UP MAIL FORWARDING SERVICE
- [ ] TRANSFER HOMEOWNERS INSURANCE TO NEW RESIDENCE
- [ ] TRANSFER UTILITIES TO NEW RESIDENCE
- [ ] UPDATE YOUR DRIVER'S LICENSE

Moving Box INVENTORY

| ROOM: | BOX NO: | COLOR CODE: |

CONTENTS:

| ROOM: | BOX NO: | COLOR CODE: |

CONTENTS:

| ROOM: | BOX NO: | COLOR CODE: |

CONTENTS:

| ROOM: | BOX NO: | COLOR CODE: |

CONTENTS:

Moving Box Inventory

| ROOM: | BOX NO: | COLOR CODE: |

CONTENTS:

| ROOM: | BOX NO: | COLOR CODE: |

CONTENTS:

| ROOM: | BOX NO: | COLOR CODE: |

CONTENTS:

| ROOM: | BOX NO: | COLOR CODE: |

CONTENTS:

Moving Box INVENTORY

| ROOM: | BOX NO: | COLOR CODE: |

CONTENTS:

| ROOM: | BOX NO: | COLOR CODE: |

CONTENTS:

| ROOM: | BOX NO: | COLOR CODE: |

CONTENTS:

| ROOM: | BOX NO: | COLOR CODE: |

CONTENTS:

Moving Box INVENTORY

| ROOM: | BOX NO: | COLOR CODE: |

CONTENTS:

| ROOM: | BOX NO: | COLOR CODE: |

CONTENTS:

| ROOM: | BOX NO: | COLOR CODE: |

CONTENTS:

| ROOM: | BOX NO: | COLOR CODE: |

CONTENTS:

Moving Box INVENTORY

| ROOM: | BOX NO: | COLOR CODE: |

CONTENTS:

| ROOM: | BOX NO: | COLOR CODE: |

CONTENTS:

| ROOM: | BOX NO: | COLOR CODE: |

CONTENTS:

| ROOM: | BOX NO: | COLOR CODE: |

CONTENTS:

Moving Box INVENTORY

ROOM:	BOX NO:	COLOR CODE:

CONTENTS:

ROOM:	BOX NO:	COLOR CODE:

CONTENTS:

ROOM:	BOX NO:	COLOR CODE:

CONTENTS:

ROOM:	BOX NO:	COLOR CODE:

CONTENTS:

Moving Box INVENTORY

| ROOM: | BOX NO: | COLOR CODE: |

CONTENTS:

| ROOM: | BOX NO: | COLOR CODE: |

CONTENTS:

| ROOM: | BOX NO: | COLOR CODE: |

CONTENTS:

| ROOM: | BOX NO: | COLOR CODE: |

CONTENTS:

Moving Box INVENTORY

ROOM: BOX NO: COLOR CODE:

CONTENTS:

ROOM: BOX NO: COLOR CODE:

CONTENTS:

ROOM: BOX NO: COLOR CODE:

CONTENTS:

ROOM: BOX NO: COLOR CODE:

CONTENTS:

Moving Box INVENTORY

ROOM:	BOX NO:	COLOR CODE:

CONTENTS:

ROOM:	BOX NO:	COLOR CODE:

CONTENTS:

ROOM:	BOX NO:	COLOR CODE:

CONTENTS:

ROOM:	BOX NO:	COLOR CODE:

CONTENTS:

Moving Box INVENTORY

| ROOM: | BOX NO: | COLOR CODE: |

CONTENTS:

| ROOM: | BOX NO: | COLOR CODE: |

CONTENTS:

| ROOM: | BOX NO: | COLOR CODE: |

CONTENTS:

| ROOM: | BOX NO: | COLOR CODE: |

CONTENTS:

Moving Box INVENTORY

| ROOM: | BOX NO: | COLOR CODE: |

CONTENTS:

| ROOM: | BOX NO: | COLOR CODE: |

CONTENTS:

| ROOM: | BOX NO: | COLOR CODE: |

CONTENTS:

| ROOM: | BOX NO: | COLOR CODE: |

CONTENTS:

Moving Box Inventory

| ROOM: | BOX NO: | COLOR CODE: |

CONTENTS:

| ROOM: | BOX NO: | COLOR CODE: |

CONTENTS:

| ROOM: | BOX NO: | COLOR CODE: |

CONTENTS:

| ROOM: | BOX NO: | COLOR CODE: |

CONTENTS:

Moving Box INVENTORY

| ROOM: | BOX NO: | COLOR CODE: |

CONTENTS:

| ROOM: | BOX NO: | COLOR CODE: |

CONTENTS:

| ROOM: | BOX NO: | COLOR CODE: |

CONTENTS:

| ROOM: | BOX NO: | COLOR CODE: |

CONTENTS:

Moving Box INVENTORY

| ROOM: | BOX NO: | COLOR CODE: |

CONTENTS:

| ROOM: | BOX NO: | COLOR CODE: |

CONTENTS:

| ROOM: | BOX NO: | COLOR CODE: |

CONTENTS:

| ROOM: | BOX NO: | COLOR CODE: |

CONTENTS:

Moving Box INVENTORY

ROOM:	BOX NO:	COLOR CODE:

CONTENTS:

ROOM:	BOX NO:	COLOR CODE:

CONTENTS:

ROOM:	BOX NO:	COLOR CODE:

CONTENTS:

ROOM:	BOX NO:	COLOR CODE:

CONTENTS:

Moving Box INVENTORY

| ROOM: | BOX NO: | COLOR CODE: |

CONTENTS:

| ROOM: | BOX NO: | COLOR CODE: |

CONTENTS:

| ROOM: | BOX NO: | COLOR CODE: |

CONTENTS:

| ROOM: | BOX NO: | COLOR CODE: |

CONTENTS:

Moving Box Inventory

ROOM:	BOX NO:	COLOR CODE:

CONTENTS:

ROOM:	BOX NO:	COLOR CODE:

CONTENTS:

ROOM:	BOX NO:	COLOR CODE:

CONTENTS:

ROOM:	BOX NO:	COLOR CODE:

CONTENTS:

Moving Box Inventory

| ROOM: | BOX NO: | COLOR CODE: |

CONTENTS:

| ROOM: | BOX NO: | COLOR CODE: |

CONTENTS:

| ROOM: | BOX NO: | COLOR CODE: |

CONTENTS:

| ROOM: | BOX NO: | COLOR CODE: |

CONTENTS:

Moving Box / INVENTORY

ROOM: **BOX NO:**   **COLOR CODE:**

CONTENTS:

ROOM: **BOX NO:**   **COLOR CODE:**

CONTENTS:

ROOM: **BOX NO:**   **COLOR CODE:**

CONTENTS:

ROOM: **BOX NO:**   **COLOR CODE:**

CONTENTS:

Moving Box Inventory

ROOM: BOX NO: COLOR CODE:

CONTENTS:

ROOM: BOX NO: COLOR CODE:

CONTENTS:

ROOM: BOX NO: COLOR CODE:

CONTENTS:

ROOM: BOX NO: COLOR CODE:

CONTENTS:

Moving Box INVENTORY

| ROOM: | BOX NO: | COLOR CODE: |

CONTENTS:

| ROOM: | BOX NO: | COLOR CODE: |

CONTENTS:

| ROOM: | BOX NO: | COLOR CODE: |

CONTENTS:

| ROOM: | BOX NO: | COLOR CODE: |

CONTENTS:

Moving Box Inventory

ROOM: | BOX NO: | COLOR CODE:

CONTENTS:

ROOM: | BOX NO: | COLOR CODE:

CONTENTS:

ROOM: | BOX NO: | COLOR CODE:

CONTENTS:

ROOM: | BOX NO: | COLOR CODE:

CONTENTS:

Moving Box INVENTORY

| ROOM: | BOX NO: | COLOR CODE: |

CONTENTS:

| ROOM: | BOX NO: | COLOR CODE: |

CONTENTS:

| ROOM: | BOX NO: | COLOR CODE: |

CONTENTS:

| ROOM: | BOX NO: | COLOR CODE: |

CONTENTS:

Moving Box INVENTORY

| ROOM: | BOX NO: | COLOR CODE: |

CONTENTS:

| ROOM: | BOX NO: | COLOR CODE: |

CONTENTS:

| ROOM: | BOX NO: | COLOR CODE: |

CONTENTS:

| ROOM: | BOX NO: | COLOR CODE: |

CONTENTS:

Moving Box INVENTORY

| ROOM: | BOX NO: | COLOR CODE: |

CONTENTS:

| ROOM: | BOX NO: | COLOR CODE: |

CONTENTS:

| ROOM: | BOX NO: | COLOR CODE: |

CONTENTS:

| ROOM: | BOX NO: | COLOR CODE: |

CONTENTS:

Address Change Checklist

UTILITIES:

- ELECTRIC
- CABLE/SATELLITE
- GAS
- SECURITY SYSTEM
- PHONE
- INTERNET
- WATER/SEWER
- OTHER
- OTHER
- OTHER

FINANCIAL:

- BANK
- CREDIT CARD
- BANK STATEMENTS
- EMPLOYER
- INSURANCE
- OTHER
- OTHER
- OTHER
- OTHER
- OTHER

New Provider Contacts

MEDICAL

FAMILY DOCTOR

NAME:
PHONE:
EMAIL:
ADDRESS:
WEBSITE URL:

DENTIST

NAME:
PHONE:
EMAIL:
ADDRESS:
WEBSITE URL:

PEDIATRICIAN

NAME:
PHONE:
EMAIL:
ADDRESS:
WEBSITE URL:

NOTES

New Provider Contacts

EDUCATION

SCHOOL #1:

NAME:
PHONE:
EMAIL:
ADDRESS:
WEBSITE URL:

SCHOOL #2:

NAME:
PHONE:
EMAIL:
ADDRESS:
WEBSITE URL:

SCHOOL #3:

NAME:
PHONE:
EMAIL:
ADDRESS:
WEBSITE URL:

NOTES

Start / Stop Utilities

ELECTRIC COMPANY

- NAME
- PHONE
- WEBSITE URL
- START DATE
- STOP DATE
- ACCOUNT NUMBER

CABLE / SATELLITE

- NAME
- PHONE
- WEBSITE URL
- START DATE
- STOP DATE
- ACCOUNT NUMBER

GAS / HEATING COMPANY

- NAME
- PHONE
- WEBSITE URL
- START DATE
- STOP DATE
- ACCOUNT NUMBER

Start/Stop Utilities

INTERNET PROVIDER

- NAME
- PHONE
- WEBSITE URL
- START DATE
- STOP DATE
- ACCOUNT NUMBER

SECURITY SYSTEM

- NAME
- PHONE
- WEBSITE URL
- START DATE
- STOP DATE
- ACCOUNT NUMBER

OTHER:

- NAME
- PHONE
- WEBSITE URL
- START DATE
- STOP DATE
- ACCOUNT NUMBER

NOTES:

Room Planner

ROOM:

PAINT COLORS::

COLOR SCHEME:

DÉCOR IDEAS:

FURNITURE IDEAS:

NOTES:

ROOM:

PAINT COLORS::

COLOR SCHEME:

DÉCOR IDEAS:

FURNITURE IDEAS:

NOTES:

Personal NOTES

Personal Notes

Personal NOTES

Personal Notes

Personal NOTES

Personal Notes

Personal Notes

Personal Notes

Personal Notes

Personal Notes

Personal Notes

Personal Notes

Personal NOTES

Personal Notes

Personal Notes

Personal Notes

Personal Notes

Personal Notes

Printed in Great Britain
by Amazon